Prophetic Friendship:

Friendship Matters
To Build a Foundation of
Moral Character

ZABED MOHAMMAD, PHD.

EDUCATOR & RESEARCHER
CANADA

EDITED BY

DR. K. W. CHRISTOPHERSON

PHD, MED, BED, BA.

Kids Edu Care

Library of Congress Cataloging-in-Publication Data
ISBN: 978-1-998923-21-2

Publisher
Kids Edu Care Inc.
Children's Dedicated Learning Series
Website: www.kidseducare.ca
Illustration Copyright © 2023 by
Kids Edu Care Inc.
Canada

Illustration & Design
Bee Digital

beedigital.asia

info@beedigital.asia

A NEW BEGINNING

Once upon a time in a small town of Canada,
there were two children named Sarah and Ahmed.
They were classmates and had known each other for
several years. As they entered their teenage years,
they started experiencing new emotions and
feelings. Sarah and Ahmed were excited
to explore the world and discover new things.
Little did they know that they were about to
embark on a journey that would
involve their friendship
and the boundaries of their relationship.

THE FIRST MEETING

One sunny day, Sarah and Ahmed met at the community library. They were both searching for books on various topics to learn and know more about moral development strategies. As they started talking, they discovered that they shared a common interest but did not find books on understanding and developing moral character.

So, they went to the front desk and asked them to find some books. This common bond led them to seeking knowledge together, discussing their thoughts and understanding of Islamic principles.

and realized that knowledge of Allah and His teachings was
the foundation of their faith. They inspired each other to
explore Islamic literature and deepen their understanding of
Quranic verses and Hadith.

BUILDING A FRIENDSHIP

Sarah and Ahmed began to spend more time together, not only discussing day-to-day life situations but also exploring other areas of their lives. They realized that they had similar hobbies and values.
Their friendship grew stronger day by day, and they felt comfortable sharing their thoughts and concerns with each other. By this time,
they discovered that the
Al Quran emphasizes the importance of choosing good friends who encourage righteousness and remind one another of their responsibilities towards Allah.

They pondered upon verses such as
Surah Al-Kahf, 18:28,
which states,

"Keep yourself content with those who call upon their Lord morning and evening, seeking His countenance."

ESTABLISHING BOUNDARIES

As their friendship deepened, Sarah and Ahmed became aware of the need to establish boundaries. They understood that maintaining a platonic relationship was essential to protect their faith and maintain a healthy friendship. They reminded each other of the Hadith where **Prophet Muhammad** (peace be upon him) said,

"Whoever believes in Allah and the Last Day, let him not be alone with a woman who has no mahram (male guardian) present, for the third one present will be the Shaytan (Satan)" *(Al-Tirmidhi).*

THE WISDOM OF MODESTY

Sarah and Ahmed often discussed
the significance of modesty in Islam.
They studied the Quranic verse

"Tell the believing men to lower their gaze and be modest. That is purer for them. Indeed, Allah is acquainted with what they do" (Al Quran 24:30)

and reflected on its implications.
They understood that modesty was not only about
physical appearance but also about maintaining a
respectful distance in their interactions.

RESPECTING PERSONAL SPACE

In their journey of friendship, Sarah and Ahmed
learned the importance of respecting personal space.
They considered the Hadith in which
the **Prophet Muhammad**
(peace be upon him) said,

*"Beware of suspicion,
for suspicion is the worst of false tales
and do not spy on one
another, and do not look for the others'
faults, and do not be
jealous of one another"
(Sahih Bukhari).*

They made sure to maintain healthy
boundaries and avoid unnecessary
intrusions into each other's lives.

MUTUAL SUPPORT

Sarah and Ahmed encountered
various challenges in their lives,
and they always found solace in each
other's company.
They recalled the Quranic verse

*"The believers are but brothers,
so make settlement
between your brothers"
(Al Quran 49:10)*

and understood the importance of supporting each
other through difficult times. They became each
other's confidants, offering encouragement and
assistance whenever needed.

DEVELOPING HEALTHY COMMUNICATION SKILLS

Sarah and Ahmed acknowledged the need for healthy communication in their friendship.
They recalled the Quranic verse

"And speak to people good [words]"
(Al Quran 2:83)

and understood that their words had the power to uplift and encourage. They focused on developing effective communication skills, being mindful of their tone and choice of words, and always aiming to promote positivity and kindness.

FOCUSING ON PERSONAL DEVELOPMENT

As Sarah and Ahmed continued their friendship,
they recognized the significance of personal development.
They recalled the Hadith where
the **Prophet Muhammad**
(peace be upon him) said,

*"Take benefit of five before five:
your youth before your old age, your health
before your sickness, your wealth before your
poverty, your free time before you are preoccu-
pied, and your life before your death"
(Al-Hakim).*

They encouraged each other to utilize their youth
in productive endeavors and personal growth.

BALANCING SOCIAL INTERACTIONS

As Sarah and Ahmed engaged in social activities, they recognized the importance of balancing their interactions. They recalled the Hadith where the **Prophet Muhammad** (peace be upon him) said,

*"A person is likely to follow
the faith of his friend,
so look whom you befriend"
(Sunan Abu Dawood)*

SETTING BOUNDARIES WITH OTHERS

As Sarah and Ahmed navigated their teenage years, they
encountered interactions with peers who had different values
and boundaries.
They recalled the Quranic verse

*"And it has already come down to you in the Book
that when you hear the verses of Allah [recited],
they are denied [by them] and ridiculed;
so do not sit with them until they enter into another
conversation"*
(Al Quran 4:140)

and understood the importance of
setting clear boundaries with those
who mock or deny their faith.

PEER PRESSURE

Sarah and Ahmed encountered situations where their friends
engaged in flirtatious behavior.
They were reminded of the Quranic verse

*"And do not obey the disbelievers
and the hypocrites but do not harm them, and rely
upon Allah.
And sufficient is Allah as
Disposer of affairs"
(Al Quran 33:48).*

They understood the importance of staying firm in
their faith and not succumbing to peer pressure,
choosing friendship over flirtation.

Sarah and Ahmed reminded each other of the
Hadith where the **Prophet Muhammad**
(peace be upon him) said,

"Actions are judged by intentions"
(Sahih Bukhari).

They understood that having pure intentions was crucial in maintaining a righteous friendship. They sought to strengthen their bond for the sake of Allah and to support each other on the path of righteousness.

GRATITUDE

Sarah and Ahmed learned the value of expressing
gratitude for their friendship.
They recalled the Quranic verse

*"And [remember] when your Lord proclaimed,
'If you are grateful, I will surely increase you
[in favor]; but if you deny, indeed,
my punishment is severe'"
(Al Quran 14:7).*

They thanked Allah for blessing them with a loyal and
supportive friend and expressed their gratitude to each
other for the positive influence they had in their lives.

SEEKING KNOWLEDGE TOGETHER

Sarah and Ahmed realized the importance of seeking knowledge together. They studied the Hadith where the **Prophet Muhammad** (peace be upon him) said,

"The seeking of knowledge is obligatory for every Muslim"
(Sunan Ibn Majah).

They embarked on a journey of learning, attending Islamic lectures and classes, and discussing their newfound knowledge, deepening their understanding of Islam and strengthening their bond.

RESPECTING DIFFERENCES

Sarah and Ahmed encountered situations where they had differing opinions on certain matters. They reminded each other of the Quranic verse

"And hold firmly to the rope of Allah all together and do not become divided"
(Al Quran 3:103)

and understood the importance of respecting each other's perspectives while staying united in their faith. They valued the diversity within their friendship and saw it as an opportunity for personal growth.

SUPPORTING EACH OTHER'S DREAMS

Sarah and Ahmed encouraged and supported
each other's aspirations. They celebrated each other's
achievements and provided guidance
and motivation when setbacks occurred.
They remembered the Quranic verse

in Surah Ash-Shura, 42:38,
"Those who have responded to their Lord
and established prayer and whose affair is
[determined by] consultation among
themselves."

CHALLENGING TEMPTATIONS

As teenagers, Sarah and Ahmed faced various temptations that tested their faith and friendship. They turned to the Quranic verse

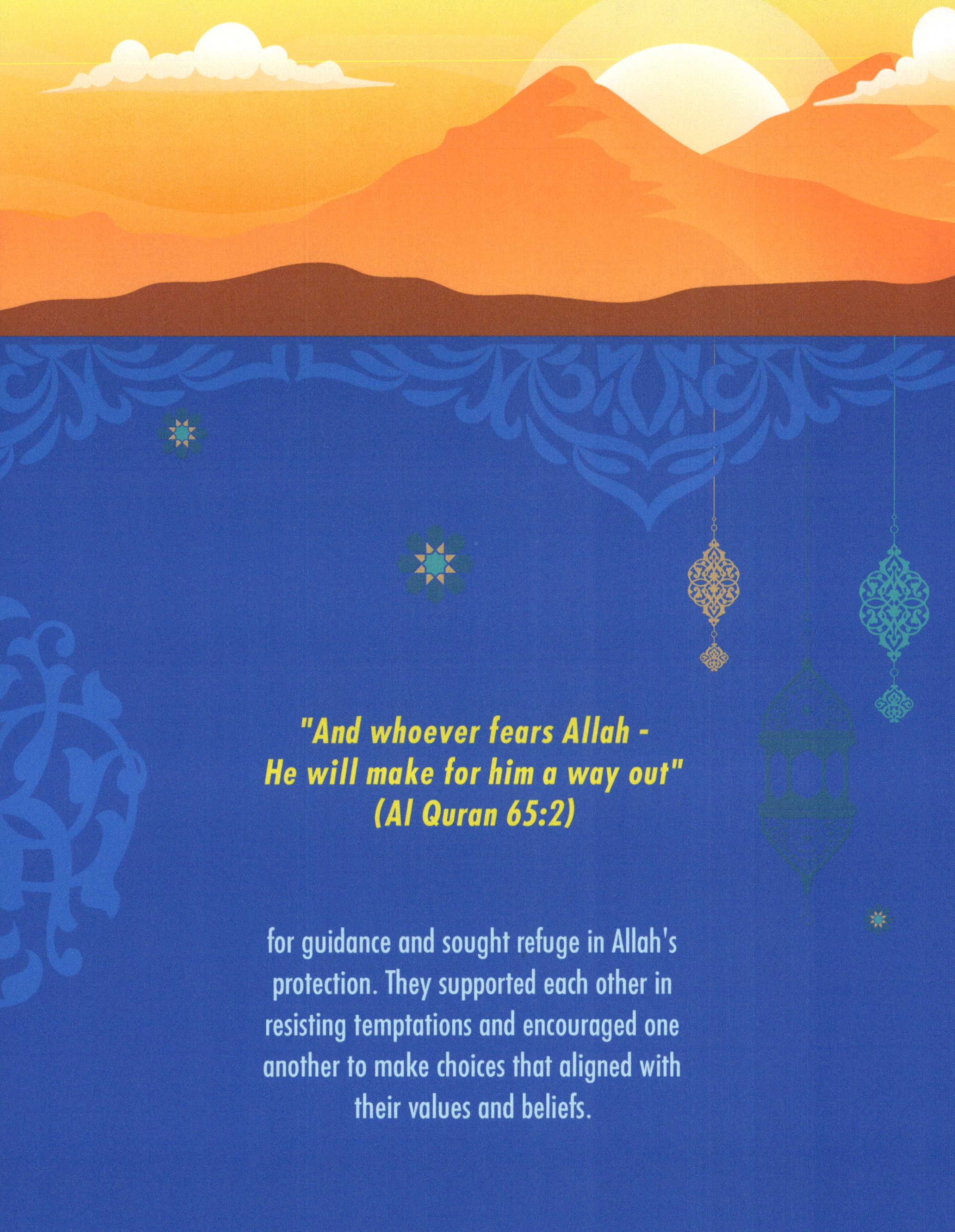

for guidance and sought refuge in Allah's protection. They supported each other in resisting temptations and encouraged one another to make choices that aligned with their values and beliefs.

MODESTY IN SPEECH AND ACTIONS

Sarah and Ahmed reflected on the Hadith where
the **Prophet Muhammad**
(peace be upon him) said,

"Modesty is a branch of faith"
(Sahih Muslim).

They understood that modesty should be reflected not only in their
appearance but also in their speech and actions. They made a conscious
effort to choose their words carefully and maintain a respectful
and dignified manner in their interactions.

SEEKING GUIDANCE FROM ELDERS

Sarah and Ahmed acknowledged the wisdom of
seeking guidance from their elders. They recalled the
Quranic verse

*"And lower to them the wing of
humility out of mercy and say,
'My Lord, have mercy upon them as they brought me up
[when I was] small"
(Al Quran 17:24)*

and respected the advice and guidance of their parents and
other knowledgeable individuals in matters of relationships
and boundaries.

Sarah and Ahmed recognized their imperfections
and the occasional mistakes they made in their
friendship. They recalled the Quranic verse

**"And let them pardon and overlook. Would you
not like that
Allah should forgive you?"
(Al Quran 24:22)**

and realized that forgiving each other's mistakes was essential
for a healthy and lasting relationship.
They practiced forgiveness and embraced the opportunity to grow
together.as they believe forgiveness is essential in maintaining a
healthy and lasting friendship.

ENCOURAGING GOOD DEEDS

Sarah and Ahmed motivated each other to
perform good deeds and engage in acts of
kindness. They recalled the Hadith where the
Prophet Muhammad
(peace be upon him) said,

*"The best among you is the one
who is best to his friend"
(Jami` at-Tirmidhi).*

They participated in volunteer activities,
supported charitable causes, and inspired each other to
make a positive impact on their community.

PATIENCE IN DIFFICULT TIMES

During challenging moments,
Sarah and Ahmed turned
to the Quranic verse

"And seek help through
patience and prayer,
and indeed, it is difficult
except for the humbly
submissive [to Allah]"
(Al Quran 2:45).

They reminded each other of the
importance of patience and seeking
solace in prayer. Their friendship
served as a source of strength,
helping them navigate through
tough times
'with perseverance.

PRIORITIZING EMOTIONAL WELL-BEING

Sarah and Ahmed recognized the significance of prioritizing their emotional well-being. They recalled the Hadith where the **Prophet Muhammad** (peace be upon him) said,

"None of you truly believes until he loves for his brother what he loves for himself"
(Sahih al-Bukhari)

and understood the importance of empathy and support in their friendship. They were there for each other during difficult times, offering a listening ear and emotional support.

REFLECTING ON LOVE AND RESPECT

Sarah and Ahmed reflected on
the Quranic verse

*"And of His signs is that
He created for you from yourselves mates
that you may find tranquility
in them; and He placed between
you affection and mercy"
(Al Quran 30:21)*

and discussed the importance of love and respect in
relationships. They understood that true love and
respect are rooted in fulfilling the rights of others and
treating them with kindness and compassion.

TRUSTING IN ALLAH'S PLAN

As Sarah and Ahmed continued their journey of
friendship, they realized the importance of
trusting in Allah's plan.
They recalled the Quranic verse

*"But perhaps you hate a thing and
it is good for you;
and perhaps you love a thing and
it is bad for you. And Allah Knows,
while you know not"*
(Al Quran 2:216)

and understood that Allah's wisdom surpasses their limited
understanding. They placed their trust in Him and knew that
He would guide them on the right path.

PRESERVING PURITY

Sarah and Ahmed discussed the significance of
maintaining purity in their thoughts and actions.
They pondered over the Hadith
where the **Prophet Muhammad**
(peace be upon him) said,

"Verily, Allah is pure and
He loves purity.
He is clean
and He loves cleanliness"
(Sahih Muslim).

They encouraged each other to guard
their intentions and actions,
ensuring they remained pure in their interactions.

PRACTICING SELF-CONTROL

In their journey,
Sarah and Ahmed encountered
moments of attraction and infatuation.
They reflected on the Hadith
where the **Prophet Muhammad**
(peace be upon him) said,

*"The strong man is not the
one who wrestles others; rather,
the strong man is the one who
controls himself when he is angry"
(Sahih al-Bukhari).*

They understood the importance
of self-control and made a conscious
effort to channel their emotions
in a righteous manner.

A FLIRTATIOUS ENCOUNTER

One day, while attending a school event, Sarah and Ahmed met new people. Among them was a teenager named Alex, who seemed interested in Sarah. Alex felt a pang of jealousy and wondered if their friendship was transitioning into something more.

A LASTING FRIENDSHIP

Sarah and Ahmed's friendship
had flourished through their teenage years.
They reflected on their journey and thanked Allah for the gift
of a strong and righteous friendship.
They realized that their bond had been strengthened by their
mutual dedication to Quranic verses and Hadith.
With hearts full of gratitude,
they promised to continue supporting and
inspiring each other on their journey
to seek closeness to Allah
and lead fulfilling lives as humans.